FRANKFURT A.M.

THE DISASTER OF THE
HINDENBURG

First published in the United States
by Scholastic Inc., 730 Broadway,
New York, N.Y. 10003

Published simultaneously in
Canada by Scholastic Canada Ltd.,
123 Newkirk Road, Richmond Hill,
Ontario, Canada L4C 3G5

SCHOLASTIC HARDCOVER is a registered trademark of Scholastic Inc.

Library of Congress Cataloging-in-Publication Data
Tanaka, Shelley.
    The disaster of the Hindenburg: the last flight of the greatest airship
ever built / by Shelley Tanaka
        p. cm.
    Includes bibliographical references.
    Summary: Describes the last voyage of the zeppelin, or airship,
Hindenburg, which crashed in flames on a New Jersey airfield in 1937,
and examines some possible causes for the disaster.
    ISBN 0-590-45750-0
    1. Hindenburg (Airship) — Juvenile literature. 2. Aeronautics —
Accidents —1937 — Juvenile literature. [1. Hindenburg (Airship)
2. Airships. 3. Aeronautics — Accidents.] I Title.
    TL659.H5T36 1993
    363.12' 465 — dc20   92–39434 CIP AC

Produced by Madison Press Books
40 Madison Avenue, Toronto, Ontario
Canada M5R 2S1

Printed in the U.S.A.
First Scholastic printing, October 1993

DESIGN AND ART DIRECTION:
    Gordon Sibley Design Inc.

ILLUSTRATION:
    Donna Gordon, Ken Marschall,
    Jack McMaster, Margo Stahl

EDITORIAL DIRECTOR:
    Hugh Brewster

PROJECT EDITOR:
    Mireille Majoor

HISTORICAL CONSULTANTS:
    Dennis Kromm, John Provan,
    Dr. Douglas H. Robinson

PRODUCTION DIRECTOR:
    Susan Barrable

PRODUCTION CO-ORDINATOR:
    Donna Chong

COLOR SEPARATION:
    Colour Technologies

PRINTER:
    R.R. Donnelley & Sons Company

Endpapers: Between March 1936 and
May 6, 1937, a flight on the *Hindenburg*
was the most elegant way to travel
from Germany to Brazil and America.

Previous page: The 804-foot-long
Hindenburg was the largest object
ever to fly.

Opposite: The giant zeppelin *Hindenburg*
looms over the crowd in its hangar.

Overleaf: In 1936 and 1937 it was not
unusual for the citizens of Frankfurt to
see zeppelins passing over their city.

Although this telling of the Hindenburg
story is based on historical fact and real people,
some scenes and dialogue have been
imaginatively recreated.

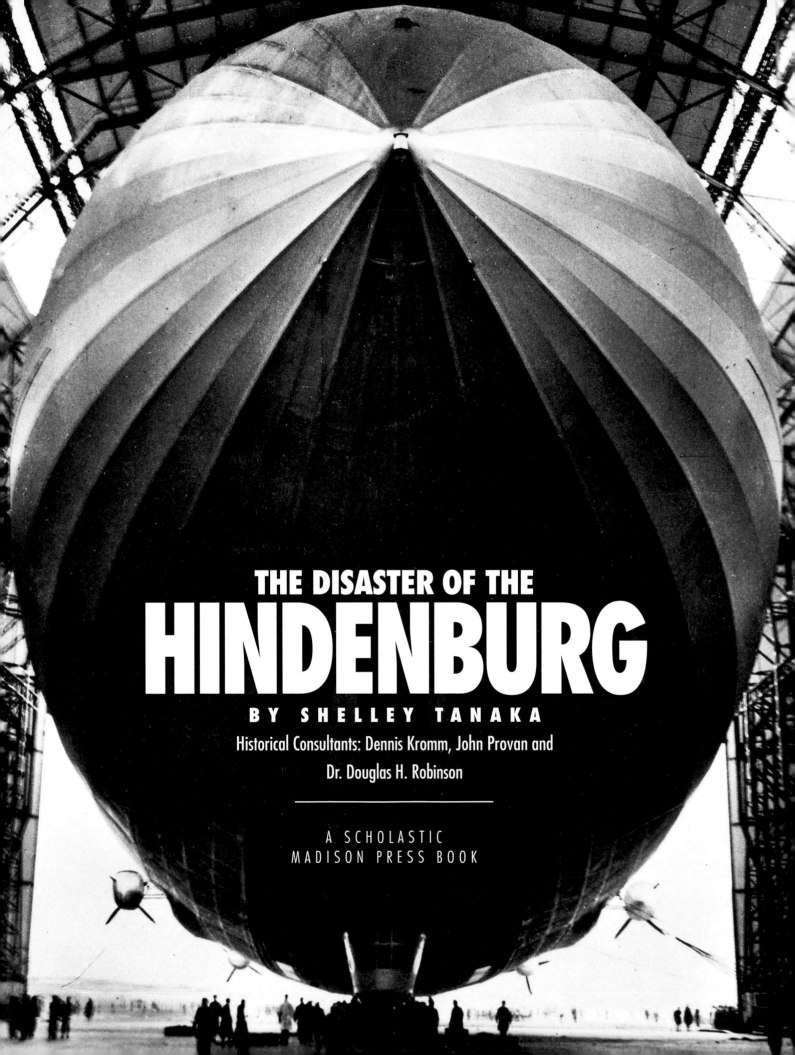

THE DISASTER OF THE
HINDENBURG

BY SHELLEY TANAKA

**Historical Consultants: Dennis Kromm, John Provan and
Dr. Douglas H. Robinson**

A SCHOLASTIC
MADISON PRESS BOOK

Contents

*To all those who died at Lakehurst
on May 6, 1937, and to the survivors, who have
lived with the memories*

T oday they hover above our cities, beaming their messages from below the clouds. Modern helium-filled blimps are quiet, safe and fuel efficient. And to fly in one of them is an unforgettable experience. But the blimps we see today are only a small reminder of a time when giant airships ruled the skies. Just sixty years ago, enormous silver zeppelins

more than forty times the size of modern blimps carried thousands of passengers around the world in style. Before the

age of the jet plane, zeppelins such as the *Hindenburg* provided the fastest and most comfortable way to cross the ocean.

And like their cousins the blimps, they offered the smoothest flight and the best view in the world.

In 1936 the *Hindenburg* is the largest and most luxurious zeppelin ever built. It is like a huge flying hotel, complete with private rooms, lounges with observation decks and gourmet dining. It regularly carries passengers from Germany to Brazil and America in record time. This is the way the rich travel, and every voyage is an event. The great airship has only one flaw: it is filled with more than seven million cubic feet of explosive hydrogen gas. The airships of the German Zeppelin Company have already flown over one million accident-free miles. But in May of 1937, thirty-two horrifying seconds will bring the age of the giant zeppelins to an end.

Prologue

August 21, 1990

Whale researcher Sara Ellis (above) scans the ocean from the gondola of a blimp. Using blimps like the one shown above, Jim Hain's team can hover above the ocean and observe whales for hours.

G LIDING SLOWLY OVER THE BLUE ocean, in a cloudless sky, the chubby blue and white blimp looks like an exotic tropical fish floating in its sea of air. So different from a streamlined plane, the MetLife airship seems out of place over the Atlantic. Normally the blimp's business is to hover over a sports stadium, its TV cameras trained on the football or baseball game below.

But this blimp is on an important mission. In addition to its pilot and co-pilot, it carries a video camera, still cameras, a tape recorder and three scientists.

Jim Hain and his associates Sara Ellis and Bob Kenney are marine biologists. They are cruising along the Atlantic coast looking for whales.

As the airship flies a zigzag course up the coast, Jim, Sara and Bob scan the water below them. The ocean appears empty, and the hours tick by. Metropolitan Life has donated five hours of flying time today. If nothing appears, they'll be "skunked" — a precious day of valuable air time lost.

Then, off to the right, a splash breaks the water. Deftly, the pilot turns the wheel, the airship approaches the spot and then drops to about 700 feet above the water. The engines are cut, and the blimp hovers quietly, and waits.

A few minutes later, right below them, a sleek humpback whale leaps out of the water. "We've got one!" Jim calls out.

Immediately, the video camera, mounted on a tripod at an open window, is trained on the water below. The video camera is switched on, still cameras are focused and pens fly over notebooks.

As the scientists watch, the whale dives below the surface and begins to move in a circle. Under the water the swimming whale begins to exhale or "blow" in short, rapid bursts. In a few seconds the underwater blows rise to the surface like columns, forming a large circular shape in the water. Soon, the scientists know, the whale will rise up in the center of this "corral" of bubbles and feast on the fish trapped inside. Suddenly Jim Hain calls his colleagues over to his window. "Look, there's another one!" Everyone crowds around to watch as a second whale begins to feed beside the first one. From the motionless blimp the team is able to watch and photograph something rarely seen: two whales feeding inside a bubble net.

"An airship can hover quietly for a long time, which makes it perfect for studying whales," says Jim, who has made about twenty airship flights since the whale project began in 1989. "It can keep pace with a swimming whale, or you can 'park' it in the air to take photographs. Observing whales from a plane can be a real neck-snapping experience if you see something interesting. A plane goes so fast that often you've already traveled a mile before you can even turn the thing around."

Jim and his team are now using blimps to help them study the small population of right whales in the North Atlantic. Right whales (so called because they were once the "right" type for hunting) are the most endangered species of large whale in the world. From an airship, Jim and his team can study the whales' migration routes, their wintering and calving grounds, and their feeding, swimming and diving behavior.

"These whales often swim in shipping lanes," says Jim, "which are becoming busier all the time. We can see how good whales are at getting out of the way of ships, and recommend changes to traffic lanes or ship speeds

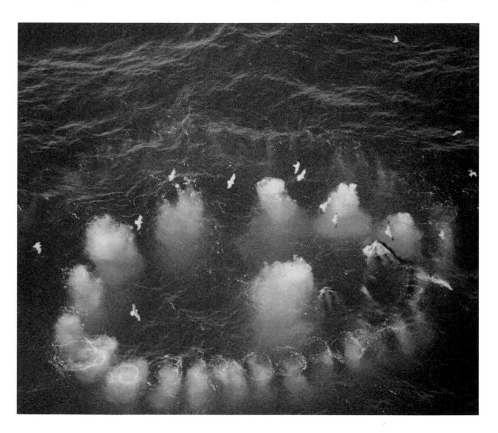

This photograph, taken from a research blimp, shows something seldom seen by humans: two whales feeding on fish trapped inside the net of bubbles created by one of the pair.

that might make things easier for them. Only about ten right whale calves are born in the North Atlantic each year, so if even a few of them are hit by ships' propellers, their numbers can be drastically reduced."

From a slow-moving or "parked" airship, researchers can determine the health of individual whales by observing their markings, wounds and coloring. Sometimes they can identify and photograph submerged animals. The airship provides a vibration-free platform for the cameras, and photographs don't have to be shot through glass, as they would on a plane. And because there's little noise, the animals aren't frightened, although sometimes they are curious.

"I've seen dolphins roll over, and sea turtles stretch their necks and lift up their heads to take a look at us," Jim says.

Whales are very sensitive to the changes in their environment that can be caused by pollution. We need to watch whales, count them and study them, for the sake of their health, and the health of the oceans.

Airships can help us do this. But there are fewer than thirty airships in use today, and right now scientists like Jim Hain have to rely on donated blimp time from companies like Fuji, Sea World and Metropolitan Life in order to carry out their vital research.

Yet only sixty years ago, airships were the queens of the skies. In the early 1900s, a brilliant and stubborn German count, Ferdinand von Zeppelin, invented the zeppelin airship. It had a rigid aluminum frame that contained huge bags filled with gas. The biggest zeppelin of all, the

Zeppelins were named after their inventor, Count von Zeppelin (top). (Above) The two most famous German zeppelins were the *Graf Zeppelin*, left, and the *Hindenburg*, right. Construction began on the *Hindenburg* in 1931 (left) and it was completed in 1936, in time to fly over the Berlin Olympic Games that year (below).

Hindenburg, was more than three-and-a-half times as long as the biggest passenger jet flying today and as high as a fifteen-story building. You could hide a modern-day blimp under one of her tail fins.

The *Hindenburg* could travel at speeds of more than eighty miles per hour. Full, she weighed a staggering 240 tons, yet she could cross the ocean in less than three days, twice as fast as an ocean liner. Before the days of long-distance passenger airplanes, airships were the fastest way to travel between continents.

But speed wasn't all they had to offer. A passenger once remarked that you didn't just travel in an airship, you voyaged. There was a dining room, a smoking room, a lounge with an observation deck and more than twenty-five cabins, all tucked inside the *Hindenburg*'s belly. The

zeppelin was like a flying luxury hotel, with the most spectacular view in the world.

In the 1930s the airships *Graf Zeppelin* and *Hindenburg* carried thousands of passengers across the Atlantic in style and traveled more than one million accident-free miles. Airships flew scientists north of the Arctic Circle to gather valuable information about the earth's atmosphere and magnetic field. The Norwegian Roald Amundsen, the first person to reach the South Pole, crossed the North Pole in an airship in 1926. The *Graf Zeppelin* traveled around the world, over territory explorers had never seen. It looked as though the airship was here to stay.

Then the *Hindenburg* arrived in New Jersey after her first 1937 flight to America. And in thirty-two seconds, the age of the rigid airship came abruptly to an end.

The Biggest Thing That Ever Flew

Before zeppelins were invented, people crossed the Atlantic Ocean in enormous ships like the 882-foot-long *Titanic*. But the *Hindenburg* brought the luxury of the ocean liners to the sky and made the same journey possible in half the time. Next to the *Hindenburg*, the 232-foot-long Boeing 747 airliners we cross the ocean in today look tiny. The 804-foot *Hindenburg* is still the largest object ever to fly. Tipped on its tail, the *Hindenburg* would come close to the 984-foot height of the Eiffel Tower. The great zeppelin was constructed of a rigid frame filled with gas bags inflated with flammable hydrogen gas. Modern blimps are more like giant balloons. They have no internal frame and get their shape from the pressure of the non-flammable helium gas that fills them. Next to these man-made giants, an 80-foot blue whale might be hard to spot!

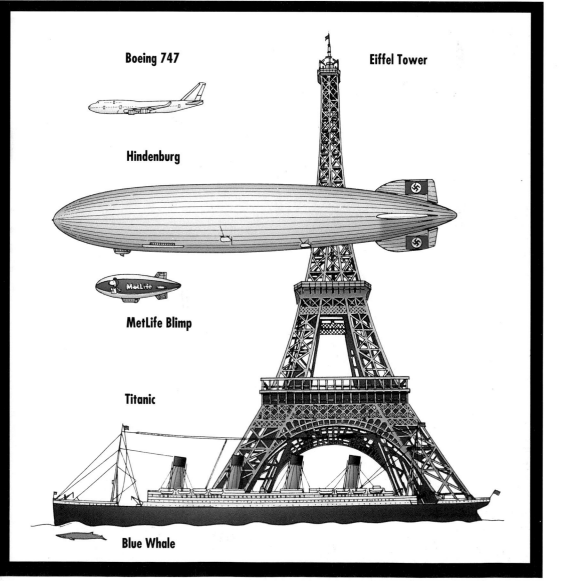

Boeing 747

Eiffel Tower

Hindenburg

MetLife Blimp

Titanic

Blue Whale

CHAPTER ONE

Boarding the Giant Zeppelin

Monday, May 3, 1937 — 7:30 P.M.

I T WAS RAINING AGAIN. SIXTEEN-YEAR-OLD IRENE DOEHNER stared out the window of the bus as it left behind the solid gray buildings of Frankfurt, Germany, and headed for the airport. It was a cheerless day for traveling, but at least she would soon be back home in Mexico. Just in time for the rainy season, she thought, as she watched the sodden countryside slide past.

Irene's father had been on a business trip, and the family had come with him to visit relatives. But Germany was a tense place to be these days. The new leader, Adolf Hitler, was becoming ruthless about expanding his power. Anyone who didn't support him one hundred percent was seen as a traitor.

"Irene, when are we going to get there? It's past supper time." Eight-year-old Walter Doehner leaned across the aisle and pulled on his sister's sleeve. Beside him, six-year-old Werner was almost asleep, his chin bobbing over the head of the stuffed teddy bear he clutched to his chest.

"They said the bus ride from the hotel wouldn't last more than a half hour," Irene said, looking at her watch.

"We should be there soon." She peered through the drizzle-splattered window. "Look, there's the airfield now. I can see the big hangar."

In less than an hour the Doehner family would leave for America on the *Hindenburg*, the biggest and most luxurious airship in the world. Mr. and Mrs. Doehner had been looking forward to the trip for weeks, but Irene was less enthusiastic. She had seen photographs of the ship, and it looked like little more than a fat squashed balloon — a ridiculous way to travel across the ocean.

Then she saw it.

The giant zeppelin lay ahead of them in the shadow of its hangar, tethered to the ground like a great silver beast. It looked impossibly huge even from a distance. As the bus pulled closer, it loomed larger still.

The bus came to a stop, and the rest of the passengers hurried to get off. The aisle filled up while Irene slowly buttoned up her coat. She couldn't take her eyes off the enormous airship.

They were all going to live inside that monster for two and a half days? This

(Above) The *Hindenburg* in its hangar at Frankfurt. Though the *Hindenburg* was bound for America on May 3, 1937, it also flew regularly to Brazil, as shown in this poster (opposite).

Before boarding the giant airship (opposite) passengers attached Zeppelin Company luggage tags (right) to all their baggage. The company also provided stickers showing the first letter of each passenger's last name (left) so that when the crew unloaded the luggage, it could be sorted alphabetically, making it easier for its owners to find.

giant gas bag was going to carry nearly one hundred people over the stormy Atlantic to the United States? More than ever she wished her parents had decided to make the return trip on the *Queen Mary*. An ocean liner floating across the sea was normal. The thing in front of her looked more like a creature from another world than a means of transportation.

Irene followed the crowd into the terminal. They had already spent three hours sitting around a Frankfurt hotel while officials searched everyone's luggage endlessly. Now there were more lineups, more inspections.

"Passport, please." A man in uniform held out his hand as Irene stepped up to the counter. "And are you carrying any lighters or matches, Fraülein? Flashlights? Camera flashbulbs?"

"Flashbulbs?" Irene reached into her pocket for the small package of bulbs that went with her new box camera. "These?"

"Just a safety precaution," he said, as he took the package from her.

"But — "

"Don't worry, my dear," said a woman's voice behind her. "I'm sure you'll get everything back in perfect order."

Irene turned around and was surprised to see that the voice belonged to a grown-up who was shorter than she was. It was one of the other passengers, a small gray-haired woman with a bright grin and an American accent.

"They'll put all your confiscated belongings in a special *Hindenburg* bag," the woman said. "You can keep the bag as a souvenir when your things are returned at the end of the trip."

"But why flashbulbs?" Irene asked.

"Who knows?" The woman shrugged cheerfully. "It's just another rule. These people thrive on them. Do you know they made me pay for thirty pounds of extra luggage? I know that everything on the ship has to be as light as possible, but I weigh a good forty pounds less than the average passenger. But rules are rules. Well, they'll be sorry. I am a wretched sea traveler, but I hear no one ever feels seasick on an airship. So I intend to eat my way across the Atlantic. I'm told the meals are excellent."

The official snapped Irene's passport shut and handed it back. "Next!" he called out impatiently.

As Irene turned to leave the lineup she tilted her head to peek at the tag on the cheerful woman's suitcase. "Miss Margaret Mather," she read, "48 Via Antonia, Rome."

Miss Mather leaned over and nudged Irene on the elbow. "I haven't been bossed around like this since boarding school," she whispered. "It makes me feel positively young!"

As the two of them burst into giggles, the customs man pulled his lips into a tight thin line.

"Irene, we're getting on now. Come over here!" Her brothers stood by the door. With them was a woman in a white uniform.

"I'm Frau Emmi Imhof, your stewardess," she said, smiling. "I'll take you to the ship. Your parents will follow along shortly."

Irene looked back at her parents who were waiting for their hand luggage to be inspected yet again. One of the officials carefully examined her mother's metal knitting needles and her bag of wool. Then he poked and squeezed the boys' teddy bears, as if he were frisking them for hidden weapons.

She followed Emmi and the boys outside. The zeppelin's metal ribs showed through its gleaming outer skin. The shiny silver fabric trembled slightly in the breeze, as if the airship were breathing.

"It doesn't look very sturdy," she muttered nervously.

"I've heard that zeppelins crash all the time."

Emmi turned to her reassuringly. "Not German zeppelins. These ships are completely safe. The materials are all extremely lightweight, but that doesn't mean they're not strong. This ship can carry over one hundred tons. And you won't feel so much as a ripple while we are in the air. It's the most wonderful feeling in the world. Believe me, this is an experience you will never forget."

Ahead, stairs led up into the belly of the ship. A small brass band blared out patriotic German songs. This was an occasion, after all. After last year's successful season of travel, the *Hindenburg* was making the first of its 1937 flights to North America. The ship was scheduled to make eighteen more trips this year. If this second season was a success, international airship travel would be here to stay. The Americans were even talking about launching a zeppelin fleet of their own.

They climbed the stairs to B-deck. Short hallways led to the showers, washrooms and smoking room.

"You're lucky," said Emmi. "Your family has been assigned two of the new cabins. They're bigger than the regular cabins upstairs, and they have windows." She opened a sliding door. "This one is yours, Irene. Normally

you would have a roommate, but the *Hindenburg* isn't full on this trip, so you'll have it all to yourself. I'll let you settle in while I take the boys next door. They'll be sharing a big cabin with your parents."

Irene looked around. It was a cozy room with bunk beds along one wall. There was a bell pull to call the steward and switches for adjusting the heat. A small vase of daffodils stood on the table next to the bed.

She opened her bag and hung up her clothes in the narrow, curtained closet. There were no drawers for her underwear and stockings, so she decided to leave them in her bag. What luck to have her own cabin. She would have hated to share with someone who might snore all night or hog the tiny fold-down sink and mirror.

She finished unpacking and then went out into the hall to join Emmi and her brothers for the tour of A-deck. The stewardess took them up the stairs past a rather grim-looking bust of Paul von Hindenburg, the former president of Germany.

"Where's the piano?" Walter asked, as they came into the lounge on the starboard side of the ship. They had all heard about the *Hindenburg*'s baby grand piano. It was specially built of aluminum that had been covered in light brown pigskin, and it weighed only 397 pounds.

"Not on this trip, I'm afraid," said Emmi apologetically. "But Captain Lehmann, the managing director of the Zeppelin Company, decided to come along on this crossing at the last minute. He is a very accomplished accordion player. Maybe we'll be able to persuade him to play for us."

Emmi turned to continue the tour. In her wake the three Doehner children exchanged disappointed glances. German folk songs on the accordion weren't exactly their kind of entertainment.

On the port side was the dining room, the tables already set with white tablecloths, gleaming china and fresh flowers. In his rush to explore the ship, Walter brushed against a chair, knocking it askew. As she set the chair back in place, Irene noticed how light it was. She could have lifted it easily with one finger.

Every room on the *Hindenburg* was designed to be both luxurious and as lightweight as possible. The walls of the lounge (above) were made of silk and painted with a map of the world showing the routes taken by famous sailing ships and airships. On all its 1936 flights the *Hindenburg* carried a baby grand piano (top) that weighed only 397 pounds. The passenger cabins (opposite and inset) contained a fold-down table and a sink with hot and cold running water.

During the *Hindenburg*'s departures and arrivals the airfield was crowded with the family and friends of those on board (left),

as well as the many men needed to maneuver the enormous ship (top). The field cleared quickly when the *Hindenburg* dropped some of the water it carried as ballast (above) to lighten the ship and stop it from descending too quickly.

Through the large open windows that ran down each side of the ship, Irene could hear the band playing. Nearby on the field stood a group of boys wearing brown uniforms and waving Nazi flags.

Behind her, the room filled up with passengers. Mr. and Mrs. Doehner finally arrived, and Irene watched in disbelief as her mother sat down and promptly pulled out her knitting.

There was a flurry of activity at the nose of the zeppelin, and they heard the captain order "Up ship!"

Irene gripped the window ledge and waited for the lurch of lift-off. But she felt nothing. Instead it was as if the *Hindenburg* were standing still and the earth below it slowly sinking away. The people on the airfield began to shrink, until they were tiny dots on the ground. Then the zeppelin stopped rising. The four engines started up, and the giant airship began to move forward.

Irene felt a tingle in her chest. Emmi Imhof was right, she thought. This trip would be an experience she would never forget.

Though Werner Franz was only fourteen years old, he had already flown to South America three times and felt quite at home on the *Hindenburg*.

From the window of the officers' mess, fourteen-year-old Werner Franz searched the group of boys waving their flags on the airfield to see if he could spot any of his friends in the crowd. Those boys were thrilled just to witness the lift-off of the *Hindenburg*. But he was a member of her crew.

As the people on the ground grew smaller and smaller, he turned away from the window and went back to setting the tables. His was the lowliest job on the ship, but he didn't care. He liked the steady routine — setting and clearing the tables for the officers, washing the dishes, tidying the officers' rooms and making their beds, cleaning their boots and uniforms. Besides, he wouldn't be a cabin boy forever. Every chance he got, he watched the other crew members at work and learned as much as he could about the workings of the airship. One day he might even

be an elevator man — the man in the control car who guided the ship up or down. It was practically the most difficult job on the ship, but there was never anything wrong with aiming high.

Werner hungrily eyed the plates of sandwiches as he placed them on the table. Roast beef and Westphalian ham, the expensive kind. Flying seemed to give him even more of an appetite than usual. He often found himself snatching leftovers off the officers' plates, even though Chef Maier always made sure he had double helpings of everything. Maybe he was growing at last. It would be a relief to look more like a teenager than a little boy.

Werner knew how lucky he was to have a position with the Zeppelin Company. It was hard to get a job of any kind in Germany right now, and he had been desperately looking for a way to help support the family. His father was out of work, and his older brother, Günter, worked as an apprentice waiter at a hotel in Frankfurt in exchange for his room and meals and just a small amount of spending money.

So when Werner heard there was a cabin boy position available on the *Hindenburg*, he didn't dare imagine he might get it. Somehow he had managed to overcome his shyness and survive a meeting with Herr Kubis, the head steward. Then had come the nerve-wracking interview with Max Pruss, one of the *Hindenburg*'s renowned captains. But finally Werner had passed his trial period. Now he was a full-fledged member of the zeppelin team. He was making more than sixty Reichsmarks a month, and proudly giving most of that to his parents. Even Günter was impressed.

"Well, Werner, are you ready for your first visit to America?" Willy Speck, the ship's chief radio officer, opened the door and poked in his head.

"Jawohl, Herr Speck."

"Good. Just remember to keep a firm hand on your

wallet while you're staring up at all those skyscrapers. New York is the most exciting city in the world, but it's a gold mine for pickpockets." The older man ruffled the boy's hair affectionately and then headed down the corridor to his post in the radio room.

Werner smoothed back his hair and smiled. Usually he hated being treated like a kid by the rest of the crew, but Willy Speck was like a father to all the men. He had been flying with the Zeppelin Company for twenty-nine years. This would be his six-hundredth trip. Herr Speck had traveled around the world on airships. He had seen herds of reindeer gallop over the arctic tundra. He had flown through the thick smoke of forest fires in Russia and cruised over the streets of Tokyo, Japan.

Some day, Werner thought, he would explore the far reaches of the world, too. He had already been to South America three times, flying over untouched stretches of tropical rainforest. In three days he would set foot in the United States of America for the first time. The best was still to come.

"OH, MOTHER..." IRENE ALMOST STAMPED HER FOOT IN frustration, but there was no arguing with her mother's stern look.

It was only eleven o'clock. After lift-off the passengers had been served a late supper of cold meats, salads and hot biscuits. The Doehner boys had nearly fallen asleep in their plates and were put to bed right after the meal. Now the lounge was filled with people watching the night view from the windows, or sitting around in sociable groups chatting and having drinks. True, most of the passengers were boring-looking businessmen, and there were no other young people on board, but it still didn't seem

(Above) Every night passengers could leave their shoes in the hallway to be shined, exactly as they would in a fine hotel. Smokers gathered in the specially sealed smoking room (opposite), where drinks were served until the last passenger went to bed.

fair. The evening was just beginning, and she was being ordered to bed like a child.

Slowly, Irene walked over to the stairs. As she gazed down the hall that led to the cabins on A-deck, she was surprised to see that many passengers had already turned in. Pairs of shoes were neatly lined outside some of the doors, waiting to be polished overnight by the steward. For a moment she considered tiptoeing down the hall and switching all the shoes around. But she changed her mind. She was sixteen years old, after all, no matter how her parents treated her.

Downstairs, other passengers were heading for the smoking room and bar. Irene had heard all about the tightly sealed smoking room with its airlock entrance and single electric lighter chained to the wall. It seemed like such an exotic, grown-up den. No doubt that's where all the good fun on the ship was taking place, but her father had told her that only men were welcome in there.

In her cabin, she undressed quickly, turned out the light and snuggled under the thick eiderdown on the top bunk. If she rested her chin on the edge of the bed, she could see out the narrow sloping window. The ship had followed the Rhine River north, and just before supper they had seen the lacy spires of Cologne cathedral silhouetted against the city lights.

Now they were floating over Holland, heading toward Belgium and the North Sea. Below her, villages looked like tiny blossoms of lights. As the giant airship cruised over the countryside, its searchlight lit up the canals and meadows below.

It was like watching a living map, she thought. If only geography class could be as wonderful as this.

CHAPTER TWO

The Luxury Liner of the Air

Tuesday afternoon, May 4, 1937

IRENE STOOD BY THE STAIRWAY ON A-deck and examined the map that charted the *Hindenburg's* progress. They still had a very long stretch of ocean to cross.

She had spent most of the morning in the lounge, playing bridge with her parents and Miss Mather, the American she had met at customs.

The sky was overcast, so there wasn't that much to see out the window, though they had passed over a couple of fishing boats and freighters that had blown their whistles at the great airship.

Now her father, like many of the grown-ups, had gone for a nap. Her mother, as usual, was knitting in the lounge.

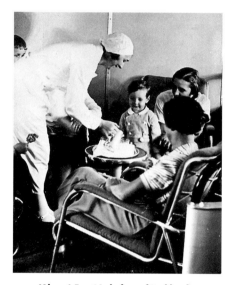

(Above) Emmi Imhof was hired by the Zeppelin Company in 1936 to help make the flight more comfortable for the many women and children then traveling by zeppelin.

Irene looked at her watch. It was a long time before she could get ready for supper. Miss Mather had invited her to join her table, remarking that there were so few female passengers on board that the women had best stick together. Irene was looking forward to it. Dining with grown-ups wasn't usually her idea of a good time, but then, Miss Mather wasn't like other grown-ups.

"How are you enjoying the trip so far?" Emmi Imhof asked as she came up the stairs. She was followed by Irene's younger brothers. Since boarding the ship they had practically glued themselves to Emmi, and the friendly stewardess didn't seem to mind a bit.

"It's fine. But are you sure there are no movie stars on board? I thought there were always famous people traveling on the *Hindenburg*."

"No film stars or lords and ladies on this trip, I'm afraid," Emmi laughed. "Although I'm told one of the passengers, Mr. Joseph Späh, is quite a well-known stage actor and an acrobat, too."

Irene smiled. She had seen Mr. Späh hamming it up and doing imitations of Adolf Hitler. Many of the passengers obviously felt some of his routines were in poor taste, but Irene thought he was funny.

"We also have a multimillionaire on board," Emmi said. "And then, of course," she teased, "if you're looking for famous people, there's always me."

"You?" Irene looked puzzled.

"Yes," Emmi laughed. "According to the Frankfurt newspapers, I'm the world's very first airship stewardess."

"Checkers, Frau Imhof," whined Walter Doehner, tugging on the stewardess's arm. "Come on. You said we could play checkers."

As the Doehner boys pulled her away, Emmi called out, "If you want to see something really interesting, take the airship tour. Dr. Rüdiger is leading a group in just a few minutes."

THE TOUR BEGAN ON B-DECK. HERR RÜDIGER, THE SHIP'S doctor, pointed out the mess rooms where the crew ate. Then the passengers took turns poking their heads into the ship's kitchen with *(continued on page 28)*

(Above) The kitchen on the *Hindenburg* was one of the busiest places on the ship. Cooks rose early to prepare breakfast for the passengers (left) and the crew. A dinner menu (right) might offer soup, duckling, venison and sole, along with a selection of cheeses for dessert.

AN BORD
DES LUFTSCHIFFES *Hindenburg*

DEUTSCHE
ZEPPELIN-REEDEREI

Speisenkarte

Die Zeppelinwerft in Friedrichshafen, die Geburtsstätte der Zeppelin-Luftschiffe

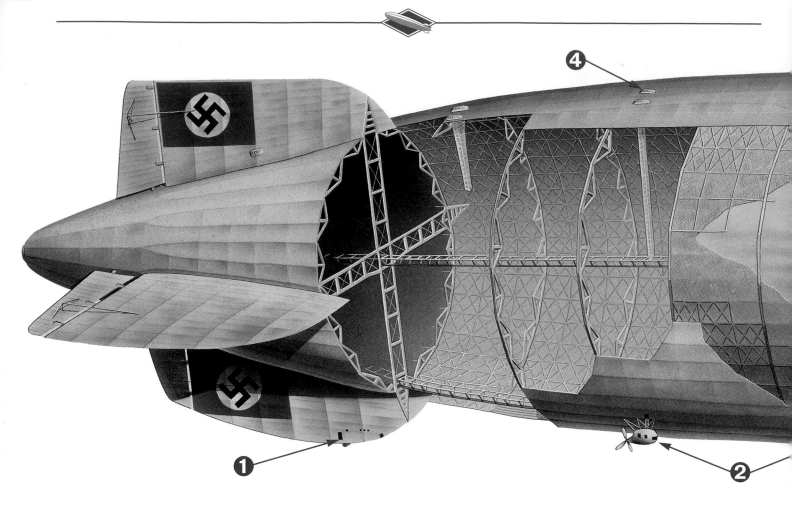

THE LUXURY LINER OF THE AIR

By 1937, German zeppelin engineers had perfected the design of the great airships. The *Hindenburg* was sleek, speedy, able to carry tons of cargo and ready to face almost any emergency.

❶ Attached to the *Hindenburg*'s enormous tail fins were the four rudders used to steer the zeppelin. Inside the bottom of the lower fin was an auxiliary control station. The captain could direct the zeppelin's flight from here if anything were to happen to the main controls.

❷ The *Hindenburg* was driven forward by four diesel engines, mounted in pairs on either side of the airship. At cruising speed, the *Hindenburg* could fly at almost ninety miles per hour. Mechanics worked in three-hour shifts so that there was always one of them inside each of the four engine gondolas to operate the engines. In case of emergencies, an extra engine was stored at the *Hindenburg*'s hangar in South America.

❸ Most of the interior of the *Hindenburg* was filled by the sixteen gas cells that gave the ship its lift. The cells were made of cotton coated with flexible plastic to make them gastight, and were held in place by metal bracing wires and rope netting. A walkway ran through the middle of the gas cells so that the ship's riggers could inspect them for leaks or holes.

❹ When the captain wanted to make the zeppelin heavier so it would go down, he ordered gas to be released from the gas cells. The escaping gas would travel up through one of the seven gas chimneys and blow away harmlessly behind the moving airship.

❺ Though the crew and passenger quarters on the *Hindenburg* were the largest and most luxurious ever placed on an airship, measuring 47 by 92 feet, they took up only 20% of the space inside *one* of the zeppelin's sixteen giant gas bags.

❻ The control car was the command center of the ship. From here the captain decided what course the airship would take and gave orders about its speed and direction. The control car windows also offered the best view from the ship.

❼ At the nose of the airship was a metal mooring cone, designed to lock into a mooring mast once the zeppelin was on the ground.

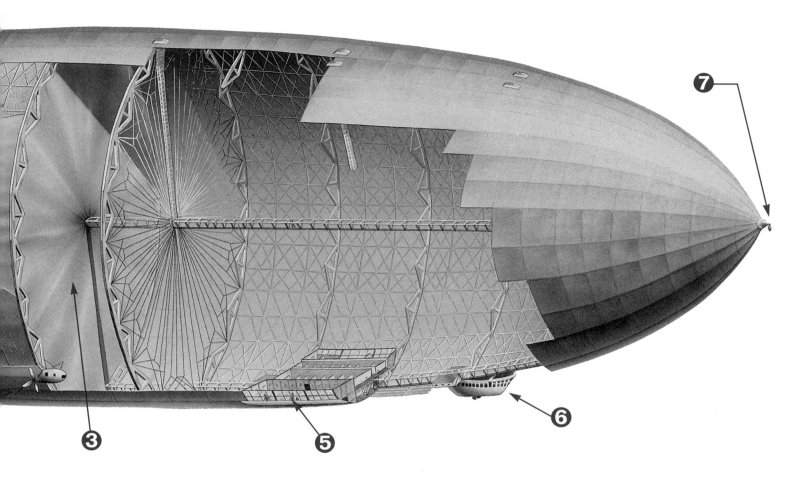

⑦

③

⑤

⑥

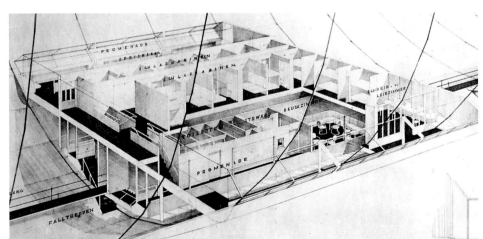

The *Hindenburg*'s designers knew that passengers would spend most of their time outside their private cabins (shown in the center of the diagram, left) in the public rooms of the ship, and so they took care to make these rooms as large and luxurious as possible. Fifty passengers could sit down for a meal in the dining room and enjoy the view from the forty-seven-foot-long windows. (Below) The sixteen enormous hydrogen-inflated gas cells that filled the interior of the *Hindenburg* gave the airship its great size and unmatched ability to lift heavy loads using very little power.

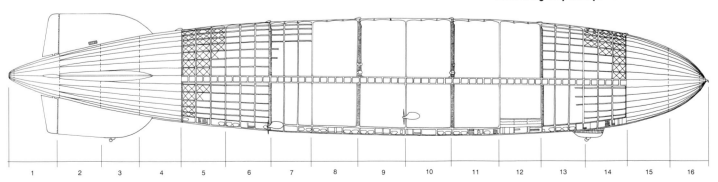

1 2 3 4 5 6 7 8 9 10 11 12 13 14 15 16

THE LUXURY LINER OF THE AIR

(continued from page 24) its electric stove, oven, refrigerator, and the little elevator that lifted food directly up to the dining room. It was amazing that the cook could prepare so many fancy meals in such a small space, Irene thought. She had woken that morning to the smell of sausages and hot buns. Someone must have to get up very early to bake hundreds of fresh rolls for breakfast.

The tour continued back toward the stern and the new passenger section where Irene's cabin was located.

"Hey," one of the passengers protested. "The cabins down here have windows."

"These nine cabins were added on during the winter," explained Dr. Rüdiger patiently. "The *Hindenburg* was designed to be inflated with helium gas. The company learned hydrogen would have to be used instead and so the ship was modified to be inflated with that gas. But after last year, so many people wanted to book flights that we decided to add these extra cabins to meet the demand. It was not a problem. Hydrogen, you see, has greater lifting power than helium."

"Greater lifting power maybe, but it is highly flammable, is it not?" asked one woman. She was composed and striking-looking, with short blonde hair and a very stylish casual outfit. Irene thought she must be a writer because she was taking notes.

Dr. Rüdiger took a deep breath, as if he were giving a lecture he had recited many times before. "Hydrogen is only dangerous if it is ignited. We have made absolutely sure this can never happen. That is why you were asked to hand over all matches and lighters before boarding. The smoking room, the only place smoking is allowed, is pressurized and tightly sealed. This makes it impossible for hydrogen to drift inside, even if it should escape from one of the gas cells. Throughout the ship, anything that could cause the slightest spark has been eliminated. The crew has been issued special felt-soled shoes to prevent static on the walkways. We have even banned flashlights or flashbulbs — anything that might cause a spark or an electric charge."

Irene nodded. Just that morning, her little brother had been running his new truck over the carpet in the lounge. The head steward thought the truck was giving off sparks,

(Above) The *Hindenburg* was under construction when this photo of its tail section was taken, so the gas cells seen at the top were not yet fully inflated. Two walkways ran through the center of the airship. One was at the bottom of the ship (top right), the other ran through the middle of the giant gas cells. Branching from the lower walkway were four small tunnels (right). These were used by the mechanics on their way to the four engine cars.

and immediately confiscated the toy. At the time Irene felt the whole thing was ridiculous, but now she was grateful. The staff on the ship were as watchful as hawks. Maybe it was a good thing.

Dr. Rüdiger led the group out of the passenger area and they proceeded in single file along the rubber-topped gangway that ran the entire length of the bottom of the ship. At first Irene was so busy worrying about losing her footing on the narrow walkway that she forgot to look up. When she finally did, she almost gasped in amazement.

The inside of the zeppelin rose dizzyingly above her. The shiny maze of steel-blue girders and ladders and wires surrounded her like an endless metal forest. She didn't know where to look first. Every girder and cable seemed to be attached to all of the others.

"If you laid out all these girders end to end," Dr. Rüdiger said, "they would stretch for ten miles."

From somewhere deep in the ship a dog barked, its lonely howls echoing eerily.

Between the girders hung the massive bags filled with hydrogen. Irene expected them to be plump with gas, like balloons, but the bottoms of some of them swayed limply.

Dr. Rüdiger explains to Irene that sixteen huge hydrogen-filled gas cells keep the *Hindenburg* floating in the air.

"Why are those bags a bit empty?" she blurted. "Is the gas leaking out?"

"This is what makes the zeppelin such a versatile craft," Rüdiger said proudly. "There are sixteen gas cells, and each one can be individually controlled. As the ship uses up fuel, the zeppelin becomes lighter. It rises up. Then the captain can order gas to be safely vented out of one or more bags. This makes the ship heavier and brings it back down."

"What if he wants the ship to go up?"

Dr. Rüdiger gestured to the drums that lined both sides of the walkway. "Some of these are filled with fuel. But others contain water that can be used as ballast. If the ship drops ballast, it becomes lighter. Do you understand?"

Irene nodded. Dr. Rüdiger talked a bit like a schoolteacher, but he did make it sound very simple.

"Can we go up there?" The blonde woman pointed high above them where a narrow catwalk ran right through the center of the ship.

The doctor shook his head. "That's the axial walkway. For crew only, I'm afraid."

Irene looked down. The silver covering of the *Hindenburg* looked papery thin to her. She put up her hand. "If you fell off one of these walkways, would you go right through the bottom of the ship?"

Dr. Rüdiger smiled. "No, you wouldn't. The fabric is strong enough to support a man's weight."

The passengers had a chance to peek into the crew's quarters — cozy little tents with canvas flaps for doors. Between the fuel tanks were hanging platforms filled with cargo. The ship even had its own power supply with two generators to supply electricity for the radio, kitchen, heating and lighting systems.

"In addition to these cargo platforms, there's a special hold for larger loads. The *Hindenburg* can carry a small airplane, or an automobile or two," Dr. Rüdiger boasted.

Then he led them onto a side gangway. The noise of

There was plenty of room aboard the *Hindenburg* (above) to carry this car (below), bound for South America in 1936.

the engine became ear-splitting. Before Irene knew it, she was peering out a doorway at the egg-shaped engine gondola. It looked like a stubby, wingless plane attached to the side of the zeppelin's hull. The giant propeller at the back whirled and roared. In the cab, a man wearing a flying helmet waved at her cheerfully. The wind rushed past her like a hurricane, whipping her hair out of its braids.

"That's Richard Kollmer," shouted the doctor behind her. "He's one of the twelve mechanics who stay with the four engines at all times."

Irene looked at the flimsy metal walkway that led to the engine car. Then she looked down ... into thin air. The empty gray Atlantic churned beneath her. It was a long way down. Irene gulped, took a step backwards and managed a feeble wave in return. Not for anything would she have traded places with Herr Kollmer.

The mechanics (above and left) had one of the noisiest jobs on the *Hindenburg*, but they were rewarded with a superb view (right).

Orders from the captain were shown on the telegraph dial and the mechanics adjusted the speed of the engines by moving the control lever (above).

RENE HURRIED UP THE STEPS TO A-DECK. SHE CHECKED HER watch. Seven o'clock, right on time. She straightened her new skirt and tucked a stray hair behind her ear. She'd decided to wear her hair loose for her dinner with Miss Mather. It made her look older.

She stood at the entrance to the dining room and looked for her hostess. Her family was already seated at their table. Walter and Werner began to beckon in her direction, but Mrs. Doehner kept them quiet with a sharp look. Irene noticed that her father was looking at her hair

with a frown. She gave an inward groan and prayed he would not spend the entire evening keeping an eye on her.

Miss Mather was sitting at her table with three male guests, and she waved when she saw Irene. As she wove her way across the room, Irene noticed, much to her disappointment, that only a few people had dressed up for the evening meal. She had been told dress on the airship was casual — the company didn't allow passengers to bring their heavy wardrobe trunks with them — but she had expected things to be a little more formal than this.

Some passengers had even shown up for breakfast that morning in their pajamas and robes!

The men at Miss Mather's table stood up when Irene approached. One of them, a very good-looking young man she had noticed on the airship tour, pulled out the chair beside him. His name was Peter Belin, and he was a Yale graduate who was now studying at the Sorbonne in Paris.

As the stewards took drink orders, Irene admired the ivory-white china and silver cutlery in front of her. The linen tablecloth was glossy and crisp. It wouldn't take much of a tilt in the ship to send the crystal glasses sliding to the floor, she thought nervously, imagining a sea of red wine in her lap.

"Isn't this lovely?" Miss Mather said, adjusting one of the stems in the vase of fresh flowers. "If I were on a steamship right now, I would be hanging over a bucket in my cabin. But flying on the *Hindenburg* is like floating on a cloud. I haven't once felt the least bit queasy." She sat back happily and examined the dinner menu. "Shall I have the veal or the ham and asparagus tonight, I wonder." She chuckled wickedly. "Or perhaps both."

"There is another great advantage over steamship travel, you know," drawled Peter Belin. "This airship can only accommodate seventy passengers, which keeps it extremely exclusive. You won't find yourself sharing the deck with people from steerage. Of course, at four hundred dollars one way, you're not going to see many budget-minded travelers on the *Hindenburg* anyway, are you?"

Irene was surprised. Four hundred dollars was a lot of money. Her father's car had cost less than that.

"They say the future of long-distance passenger travel lies with airplanes," said an American man who was sitting beside Miss Mather. "One day we'll be flying across

(Opposite) Mealtime on board the *Hindenburg* was a special event. Each table was carefully set with Zeppelin Company china and silverware (left and right) and decorated with fresh flowers. White-coated stewards would serve the food, and passengers could choose from French or German wines. After their flights, passengers would sometimes take plates home as souvenirs. The silk walls of the dining room (above) were decorated with scenes from the *Graf Zeppelin*'s flights to South America.

the ocean in a matter of hours, not days. Besides — "

"Well, I'm a licensed pilot, myself," interrupted Peter, "and I have done a great deal of research into zeppelins. Don't forget those nets in the hold are filled with thirteen tons of freight, including thousands of cards and letters. All money-makers. A DC-3 can carry twenty passengers

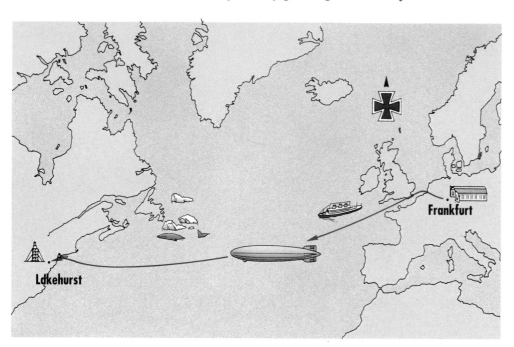

The *Hindenburg* flew from Frankfurt, Germany, to Lakehurst, New Jersey, in two and a half days — less than half the time the journey would take by ocean liner. And not one zeppelin passenger ever suffered from airsickness.

and lift about two tons. Airplanes, no matter how fast they become, will never be able to carry the payload of a zeppelin. Besides, an airship is a much more straightforward flying machine than a plane. An airplane requires huge power and speed just to get itself off the ground, let alone stay in the air. But a zeppelin rises up with no effort and then sails through the air rather than plowing through it. Simple and elegant."

Irene nodded. She had never been able to understand how airplanes, those heavy, clunky lumps of metal, stayed up in the sky.

"I can't imagine a day when people will be in such a hurry that they would give up the luxury of airship travel to sit in a cramped airplane," Miss Mather agreed. "Those tin boxes are noisy enough to rattle the brains right out of your head. But here you can barely hear the engines."

Peter Belin reached for his empty wine glass and examined it critically. Appearing to notice a smudge, he picked up his linen napkin to polish the glass. From

nowhere appeared one of the stewards, Wilhelm Balla, who deftly whisked the glass out of Peter's hand and put a fresh one on the table.

Peter looked a bit startled at first. Then he smiled. "Attentive service, I must say," he murmured appreciatively. "These Germans are well trained."

Irene looked up at Wilhelm, who was already expertly uncorking the wine. He glanced at her, and she was sure she saw him roll his eyes.

She stifled a giggle. Peter Belin was a terrible snob, but who cared? She was having fun for the first time on the trip.

DEEP IN THE BELLY OF THE SHIP, Werner Franz was asleep in his bunk. The gentle drone of the *Hindenburg*'s engines filtered into his dreams...

Elevator man Werner Franz stands at his usual station in the control car of the Zeppelin Company's latest airship. The room is surrounded by windows, and the view in every direction is spectacular, but he pays no attention. He is concentrating completely on his duties. After years of experience, he can tell simply by feel whether the ship is nosing up or down. When it does, he turns the wheel exactly the right amount to put the ship on an even keel. He knows that if the ship tilts more than five degrees, wine bottles will fall over, and kettles full of boiling water will start to slide off the stove in the kitchen.

A man with a baggy, bloodhound face enters the control car. It is Dr. Hugo Eckener, the person who knows more about zeppelins than anyone else in the world. He is a legend to every airship man.

"Ah, I thought it was you, Herr Franz," Dr. Eckener says. "I could tell by how smoothly the ship was flying that we had the company's best elevator man at the wheel...."

A rough jostle on the shoulder woke Werner abruptly. He rolled over groggily. Wilhelm Balla sat on the bottom bunk. He was grinning up at his bunkmate.

"Sorry," Wilhelm said. "There's more room in a pup tent than there is here. Besides, you looked much too peaceful. Didn't I tell you that you would sleep like a baby in a cradle on an airship?" His deep voice boomed through the darkened ship.

"Hey, Balla! Shut up!" An angry shout came from the other side of the canvas wall that separated the crew's cubbyholes.

Werner smiled. Wilhelm was an excellent steward. He could carry an armful of plates full of steaming food across a crowded dining room without a single wobble. Yet the big man couldn't seem to get himself into bed without waking up the entire ship.

"Ja, ja, Mensch, geh mal schlafen. Go back to sleep," Wilhelm muttered crossly. But he lowered his voice.

"How was night shift?" Werner whispered, leaning back with both his arms crossed behind his head.

"Busy. There are three Luftwaffe intelligence men on board, and they demanded sandwiches at midnight. They seem to be patrolling the ship. What a waste of time. As if they would be able to find a bomb on something this size."

"A bomb?" Werner's mouth fell open.

Wilhelm shook his head. "Don't you know how unpopular Hitler has made Germany right now? There are anti-Nazi demonstrations in New York City all the time. Why do you think this ship isn't flying with helium? The Americans won't sell it to us because they think Hitler might use this ship for war. Destroying the *Hindenburg* would make him look very bad. Just two years ago someone found a time bomb on the *Graf Zeppelin*. Who says it can't happen again?" He flopped into his bunk, yawned and turned toward the wall.

Werner lay in bed listening to his friend's snores. He couldn't understand it. He just wanted to work hard and help his family. He was happy to be a member of the crew of the greatest airship in the world, the pride of Germany. He knew nothing about intelligence men or bombs.

Besides, who would ever want to destroy a beautiful ship like this?

WHEN ZEPPELINS WERE KING

The 1920s and 30s were the decades when zeppelins ruled the sky, but you didn't need to look in the air to find them. Children might receive a zeppelin Valentine (right) or a zeppelin game (above).

Even everyday objects, like this pocketknife (above), carried pictures of zeppelins. (Right) Thousands of these packages of needles in zeppelin-shaped envelopes were sold in America.

CHAPTER THREE

The Only Way to Fly

Wednesday, May 5, 1937

"WELL, MY DEAR, ARE YOU TELLING YOUR FRIENDS ALL about the trip?"

Irene looked up from the writing desk. Margaret Mather was smiling at her.

"I've become a bit lazy, I'm afraid," the girl admitted, straightening the small pile of postcards in front of her. "My first six cards were full of news, but I got tired of saying the same thing over and over. Now I'm just writing 'Greetings from the *Hindenburg*,' on each one."

"I don't blame you a bit." Miss Mather glanced at the man sitting at the next table. He seemed to have hundreds of postcards in front of him and was busily sticking labels on each one. "That gentleman has the right idea," she whispered. "He had his secretary type up address labels before he left Germany. He probably has a stamp with his signature on it, too, so he doesn't even have to sign the things. Besides, it's a shame to spend the trip buried in correspondence when you could be enjoying the view." She pointed through the door of the writing room to the observation deck windows, and Irene frowned for a

The airship's writing room (left and opposite) offered passengers a quiet place to write cards and letters. (Right) Zeppelins worked as part of the German airmail service. The card, above, was postmarked in Frankfurt and dropped to the ground for mailing as the *Hindenburg* flew over Germany on May 3, 1937.

moment, puzzled. The entire airship was surrounded by a thick blanket of cloud.

But Miss Mather was grinning. "Don't worry. It won't last forever. I'm told we are getting very close to the east coast of Canada. I'm certain there will be something to see soon."

Irene laughed. Miss Mather was old enough to be her grandmother, but you would never know it, she was so lively and easy to talk to.

Lying on her bunk late the night before, Irene had relived every minute of that evening's supper. Miss Mather had told them all about her travels to Greece, Africa and Albania. She was a poet, too, and lived in Rome on practically the same spot where the poet John Keats had once lived. Miss Mather said Rome was the most romantic city in the world.

Irene had decided that when she was older she would be just like Miss Mather. She would stay single and free so she could travel and see the world, instead of settling down and having a family.

Her family had been the only damper on the whole evening. They had sat just two tables away, and Irene spent the whole meal trying to ignore them. The worst moment came when Peter offered her a glass of wine. Irene saw her father's eyes boring into her, so she had to grit her teeth and refuse. It was so unfair.

Still, the evening had been the highlight of the trip, so elegant and sophisticated.

"Thank you again for inviting me last night, Miss Mather," she said now.

"I'm glad you enjoyed yourself. Did we manage to convince you that zeppelins are the best way to fly?"

"Well, I — " Irene paused. The sound of the engines had changed. The dull roar became muffled and thick, and she felt a slight popping in her ears. Though there was no perceptible movement, she could swear the airship was dropping.

"Did you feel that?" she asked, a worried frown coming over her face.

But Miss Mather was already moving to the windows. She turned and waved Irene over.

"Look," she said. "I told you there would be something to see."

Irene joined her beside the wide panes. The ship had

moved beneath the cloud cover, and was now hovering low over the Atlantic so the passengers could see the view below them.

"Icebergs!" Irene had always imagined they would look like giant bobbing ice cubes, but this was nothing like that. Floating white mountains rose majestically out of the black ocean. They looked still and massive — beautiful and frightening at the same time.

As they watched, a ragged cliff seemed to break off the side of a huge berg in slow motion, tumbling into the sea with a thundering crack that they could hear even through the closed windows of the zeppelin. A flurry of gulls exploded into the air like sparks.

"It's called calving," drawled a male voice behind them. Irene turned around as Peter Belin began snapping photographs. "A mother iceberg giving birth to a smaller one."

Nothing could match the view from the *Hindenburg*'s windows (below). On sunny days passengers could watch the huge shadow of the zeppelin (bottom) passing over the waves.

Then the sun broke through the clouds.

It was as if the craggy white landscape had been lit up from the inside. The black Atlantic became almost transparent, and the ice suddenly reflected the sunlight in unreal shades of green and blue. As Irene gazed down in awe, rainbows appeared, double ones that formed complete circles, as if drawn by an invisible hand.

"Look!" Peter shouted, pointing below them. The cool tone was gone; he sounded as excited as a little boy.

At first Irene saw nothing. Then, in an instant, two dark shapes appeared in the water, looking like slippery smooth stones breaking the surface. She blinked, and they were gone.

"What — " Before she could speak, the blue-gray mounds appeared again a little farther off. This time there were three of them,

not the chubby creatures Irene had seen in her school-books, but long slender swimmers, graceful as eels.

Whales. The sight took Irene's breath away. Even from such a great height they looked absolutely enormous.

"Blue whales," Peter breathed. "They seem to prefer to live along the edge of the ice. Bigger than any animal that has ever lived on the earth, you know, including the dinosaurs. What a sight."

The giant shadow of the *Hindenburg* fell over the whales, and they seemed to sense it, slipping along below the surface of the water even faster, as if challenging the zeppelin to a race.

Can they see us? Irene wondered. Are they frightened by this huge monster coming out of the clouds, like a creature from another world? Or do they think we're one of them — a big silvery fish floating in the ocean of sky?

Below, one of the creatures surfaced and spouted an immense heart of spray, as if in greeting. Without thinking, Irene raised her hand and waved back.

"Well, my dear, what do you think of airship travel now?" Miss Mather said softly.

Irene opened her mouth to speak, but no words came out. Miss Mather nodded. She knew exactly what Irene was thinking.

There was no longer any doubt in her mind. Airships were the only way to travel.

WERNER FRANZ WALKED INTO THE OFFICERS' MESS WITH another pot of coffee. The room was unusually quiet. Most of the men had finished their coffee quickly and returned to their stations. Now there were only Captain Pruss and Captain Lehmann with one of the passengers, a Colonel Erdmann. Wilhelm said Erdmann was chief of special intelligence with the German Luftwaffe. Until now, Werner wasn't sure he believed him.

The men were huddled at the far table, all deep in conversation. Werner went to put the coffee in front of them, but Captain Pruss waved him off brusquely.

Werner backed away quietly. Something was afoot. The captain almost always had a kind word for every member of the crew, even a lowly cabin boy.

Werner had never seen Captain Pruss so preoccupied. Everyone knew the ship was running almost a half day late due to the headwinds, but storms weren't unusual at this time of year, and they had experienced delays before. What was going on? Did this have something to do with Wilhelm's bomb story?

Chef Maier poked his head in the door. "Werner," he ordered. "I need some more eggs. Bring me four dozen, would you?"

"Jawohl, Herr Maier." Werner hurriedly stacked the rest of the dishes and left the room, sliding the door quietly closed behind him.

He stepped onto the gangway leading into the hold and took a deep breath. He loved it back here. It was like being in the cozy belly of a giant whale. The enormous gas cells were like the lungs that kept the zeppelin beast alive and

Captain Ernst Lehmann (left) and Captain Max Pruss (right) were two of the Zeppelin Company's most experienced commanders. Though Lehmann was often photographed with his pipe, he never lit it while on the *Hindenburg*.

afloat. Around him, daylight filtered through her silvery smooth skin stretched tight over the skeleton of those massive metal girders. As she skirted along the side of a storm, she could gobble up rainwater for ballast. Her finely tuned

The *Hindenburg's* captains directed the zeppelin's flight from inside the control car (above). In the chart room (right) they determined their position and mapped the course the airship would take.

engines hummed as regularly as a heartbeat.

Werner headed back to the food storeroom to fetch the eggs. The trip was almost over and there were still massive piles of food left — hundreds of bottles of wine and mineral water, big wheels of cheese, lumpy packages of smoked meat.

He found the eggs, turned off the light and headed back to the kitchen. As he stepped onto the gangway, he saw a sudden movement. Someone was tucked between two water tanks, hiding.

It was one of the passengers, Mr. Späh. Werner had heard all about him. A nuisance passenger, the crew

called him. He was a comedian of some kind, famous for his imitations of rubber-legged drunks and his side-splitting anti-Hitler jokes.

"Can I help you with something, sir? Passengers are not supposed to be in this part of the ship unaccompanied." Werner hoped he sounded polite but authoritative.

"I was just visiting my dog," Joseph Späh said impatiently. "That's not a crime, is it? Or are the Nazis recruiting cabin boys now to spy on passengers." He looked at Werner's astonished face and then softened. "Look, I'm not doing any harm. Ulla won't eat unless I'm there with her. I'm taking her home to my kids, and I don't want to show up with a half-starved animal. You can understand that, can't you? How old are you, anyway?"

"Almost fifteen," Werner said, drawing himself up.

"Ever been to New York?" Werner shook his head. "Well, you'll love it. If you get a chance, go to Radio City Music Hall. Biggest theater in the world. I'll be playing there myself soon. Come and catch my act." He reached into his pocket and drew out a crisp American five dollar bill. "Here. Buy yourself something special. My treat."

Werner looked at the money longingly. It was almost two weeks' salary for him.

He shook his head. "We're not allowed to accept tips, sir. Company regulations."

Mr. Späh snapped the bill back into his pocket and shrugged. "And you always do what you're told, no matter what, right?" Then his face became serious.

"Fifteen, eh?" he said softly. "You've got your whole life ahead of you. Take my advice, kid. Get out of Germany. I used to be a German citizen myself, but I'm an American now. Your leader, Hitler, is a madman. He will bring great evil to the world. Unless somebody stops him first."

The small man turned and hurried on down the hallway as Werner stared after him, his head spinning.

For the first time in his short airship career, he began to look forward to the trip coming to an end.

THE PRIDE OF THE REICH

The Zeppelin Company flag (below) showed an airship circling the globe above a swastika, the Nazi symbol.

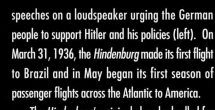

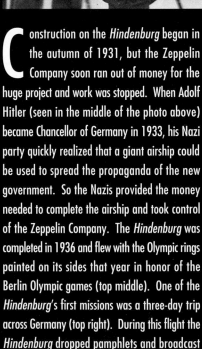

Construction on the *Hindenburg* began in the autumn of 1931, but the Zeppelin Company soon ran out of money for the huge project and work was stopped. When Adolf Hitler (seen in the middle of the photo above) became Chancellor of Germany in 1933, his Nazi party quickly realized that a giant airship could be used to spread the propaganda of the new government. So the Nazis provided the money needed to complete the airship and took control of the Zeppelin Company. The *Hindenburg* was completed in 1936 and flew with the Olympic rings painted on its sides that year in honor of the Berlin Olympic games (top middle). One of the *Hindenburg*'s first missions was a three-day trip across Germany (top right). During this flight the *Hindenburg* dropped pamphlets and broadcast speeches on a loudspeaker urging the German people to support Hitler and his policies (left). On March 31, 1936, the *Hindenburg* made its first flight to Brazil and in May began its first season of passenger flights across the Atlantic to America.

The *Hindenburg*'s original plans had called for the airship to be inflated with non-flammable helium gas. However, in 1936 the only country in the world with a large supply of helium was the United States. Fearing that Hitler would use zeppelins as war machines, the U.S. government would not sell the gas to Germany. So the *Hindenburg* was inflated with hydrogen, a highly flammable gas. American fears about Hitler were later shown to be justified. Two years after the *Hindenburg* disaster Hitler's invasion of neighboring countries led to World War II and the deaths of millions of people.

CHAPTER FOUR

America at Last

Thursday, May 6, 1937 — 6 P.M.

RENE SIGHED AS SHE STARED AROUND the observation deck. Would they never land? The *Hindenburg* had been fighting bad weather for the whole trip, and now it was twelve hours late. So much for crossing the Atlantic in two and a half days.

She couldn't understand why it was taking so long. They had circled the Lakehurst airfield two hours ago in a gray rain that was as dreary as the one they had left behind in Frankfurt. But instead of landing, the ship continued down the coast toward Atlantic City. Her brothers loved watching the ocean surf beating against the piers, but Irene was tired of sightseeing. She just wanted to get there. Besides, the delay seemed to be making everyone

A passenger took the picture above left when the *Hindenburg* reached America on May 6, 1937. That afternoon the airship floated over New York (top right), a city as glamorous in real life as all the posters had promised (opposite).

tense. Captain Lehmann had arrived late for the noon meal again, and Captain Pruss looked pale and tired and barely chatted with the passengers at all. Even Mr. Späh, the funny actor, seemed moody and preoccupied now.

The stewards had served sandwiches and cleared them away, and the dining-room tables had been pushed together in preparation for customs inspection at Lakehurst. It was as if everyone thought the trip were already over.

Irene sighed again. The whole day had gone by unbearably slowly, ever since they had woken up to a dreary dawn off the coast of Nova Scotia. Since then the zeppelin had flown in and out of cloud cover all day long. The low cruise over Boston was shrouded in mist. New York City was pretty spectacular, though. The sun broke through the clouds just as they were flying over the Empire State Building, the tallest building in the world. Trolley

cars clanged their bells, and shoppers and taxi drivers stopped to gaze up at them from the streets, honking their horns and waving.

"You look bored," said a voice. Irene looked up. It was one of the other passengers, a shortish man with a friendly face.

She sat up a little straighter. "It's just that it's taking so long to get there."

"That's because there are storms about," the man said. "Didn't you see the lightning earlier?"

Irene shook her head.

"Well, the captain wants to hold off until landing conditions are a little better. These German pilots don't take any chances. That's what makes them the best." He looked down at his watch. "Hope he doesn't take too long, though. I'm pretty anxious to land myself." The man put out his hand. "I'm Burt Dolan. From Chicago. You remind me of my daughter Mary Alice. She's about your age, and she hates waiting around, too." He grinned. "My family's expecting me to arrive by steamship later this month. Will they be surprised when I walk in the door two weeks early."

"Why didn't you go by boat?" asked Irene. "It may not be as fast, but there's more to do. Shuffleboard, deck tennis, that kind of thing." Mr. Dolan looked about the same age as her father, but considerably more trim and athletic.

The American shrugged. "Friend of mine over there, Nelson Morris, convinced me to take the *Hindenburg*. He's flown on the *Graf Zeppelin*, and he said this would be faster and more comfortable than going by sea. My wife will be furious when she finds out. I promised her I wouldn't fly. She doesn't think it's safe. I'm hoping she'll forgive me, though, when I turn up in time for Mother's Day on Sunday. I haven't seen my family in six months, and I've missed them like crazy." He smiled at Irene and then reached into his briefcase.

"Here," he said. "Little souvenir for you. I've got all kinds, but this one's my daughter's favorite." He handed Irene a tiny crystal bottle of perfume.

Irene didn't know what to say. "Thank you. But are you sure — "

Mr. Dolan waved away her thanks. "No problem," he smiled. "It's my business. Hope you like it." Then he gathered up his overcoat and briefcase and went to

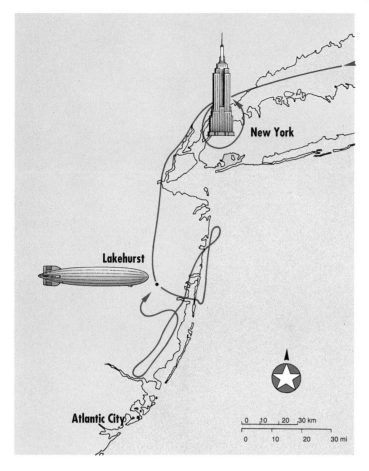

even see an American film at that place Mr. Späh had told him about.

Over the zeppelin's speaker system came the call to landing stations. In the hallway Werner could hear the crew members heading to the nose of the ship to help bring the bow of the zeppelin down and drop the landing lines during docking.

"Herr Sammt." Ludwig Knorr, the chief rigger, was calling to one of the officers. The footsteps of the two men slowed down outside the mess door. "Gas cell number four looks a little high. It could be a leak. Tell the captain we'll have to check on it after we land."

"Right," the officer answered. The footsteps quickened again, and the two men hurried on to their posts.

Werner smiled. Ludwig Knorr was the company's most experienced rigger, and those gas cells were like his babies. He could tell just by placing his hand on a bag whether the pressure was right.

If he said a bag was leaking, it was leaking. And if the leak needed to be repaired, maybe there would be even more time for them in America than he had hoped.

IRENE STOOD BY THE OPEN WINDOW OF THE DINING ROOM observation deck. Mr. Doehner was down in the cabin fetching the last of the hand luggage. Mrs. Doehner sat on a bench nearby. She looked a little frazzled, loaded down with coats and scarves and her knitting bag. Werner and Walter Doehner were leaning over the window ledge watching the scene below. Their hair was slicked back and their faces were scrubbed and shiny. Irene could see the other passengers giving the boys fond glances, and even she had to admit they looked very sweet in their identical Buster Brown suits, each of them clutching a teddy bear.

The giant zeppelin had circled the airfield once more and was finally coming in to land. The sound of the engines was louder now. The rain had stopped, but the field was still spotted with puddles that gleamed when the last rays of the setting sun occasionally broke through the thin clouds.

Below her Irene could see the wide empty space of the airfield with the enormous hangar behind it and the tall triangular tower of the airship's mooring mast in front. The field was dotted with the tiny figures of the mooring party, many of them dressed in blue navy uniforms.

As the zeppelin passed over the station buildings and

join his friend on the other side of the room.

Irene pulled out the stopper of the delicate bottle and sniffed the heady fragrance. She read the tiny label printed on the bottom. The scent was called "Tailspin."

WERNER FRANZ WAS STACKING DISHES IN THE OFFICERS' mess. It was taking him longer than usual because he kept wandering over to the window to look out.

He was tense with excitement. Soon he would set foot in America, the great land of cowboys, skyscrapers and opportunity. He couldn't wait to get a closer look at New York City. When the airship had flown over the sea of tall buildings, he had been unable to tear himself away from the sight. All the famous places he had heard about — the Statue of Liberty, Central Park, Times Square. They had even passed over a sports stadium where two teams had been playing baseball. New York gleamed and soared. It was so different from drab old Frankfurt.

Tomorrow, if they could get permission, he and Wilhelm planned to go into the city and do some sightseeing. He had a small amount of money set aside to buy souvenirs for his parents and brother. Maybe he would

KEN MARSCHALL 1979

As the *Hindenburg* hovered over the sandy airfield at Lakehurst (left) a passenger leaned out the window and snapped this photograph (below)

turned to make its final approach, ballast tanks were opened to slow its descent. Water gushed out of the bottom of the ship, soaking some of the mooring party below. Walter Doehner whispered something in his younger brother's ear, and the two little boys began to cackle hysterically. Then Walter started to dance his teddy bear around the window ledge, until he ended up accidentally thwacking Irene in the shoulder with it.

"Give me that," she hissed, snatching the bear away. "You're too old for dolls, anyway." She looked around in embarrassment, but everyone was too preoccupied to pay any attention to her.

The only people who didn't seem to be watching the landing were two white-coated stewards standing against the rear wall. They chatted together casually, their arms crossed in front of them. One was the big steward, Wilhelm. When he saw Irene looking at them, he smiled and winked at her.

Blushing, Irene turned back to the window. The airship kept turning until the mooring mast lay straight ahead. They were very close now. Two mooring lines dropped from the bow and a swarm of men on the ground raced forward to grab them. Then the steel mooring cable was slowly lowered from the ship's nose. The engines became silent, and the ship stopped moving.

Everyone at the station was looking up at them, faces filled with awe. How wonderful the *Hindenburg* must look from below, Irene thought, as the ship hovered barely two hundred feet above ground. Near the hangar a cluster of reporters fiddled with their sound recorders and notebooks. In the parking lot newsreel photographers stood on the tops of cars, their movie cameras on tripods in front of them. Some people were already taking pictures, their flashbulbs popping in the fading light.

Suddenly Irene felt very proud to be on such a magnificent ship. The people on the ground began to wave, and she waved back, smiling serenely. She felt a bit like a movie star, or royalty. It was as if all these people had come out to greet just her.

Then she heard a deep thumping noise far behind her, and the ship shuddered. And as she watched, the expressions of the people on the ground abruptly changed.

of the landing crew getting ready to pick up the ropes dropped from the ship. Perhaps the photographer wondered why some of the men on the ground were turning and beginning to run away.

CHAPTER FIVE

Disaster!

Thursday, May 6, 1937 — 7:25 P.M.

WHAT WAS HAPPENING? IRENE WAS TRANSFIXED BY THE horrified stares that filled the faces of the people on the ground. They were all looking up in terror, as if the *Hindenburg* had suddenly sprung fangs and were coming down to devour them.

The people on the ground began to scream. The men in the mooring party dropped the ropes as if they were poisoned. Then they all turned and started to run away from the ship.

All at once everything was very bright, as if the sky had been switched on. The ship lurched viciously, and Irene was thrown off her feet against the railing that separated the observation deck from the dining room. She was still clutching Walter's bear.

"Mother! Walter!" But her cries were lost in the screams. She thought she could hear her littlest brother calling, but she couldn't see him. The light metal tables and chairs tumbled around the room like giant jacks. One caught her on the temple.

Irene tried to stand up, but the floor was tilted. She slid backwards on her knees, pummelled by sliding furniture and bodies. She grabbed onto the side railing to pull herself up, but it was burning hot, and she quickly let go. Everything was hot. She began to slide back again, until a strong arm reached over and pulled her up by the elbow.

It was Frau Imhof. She was sitting on the floor on her hip, her legs twisted oddly beneath her. Emmi nodded to Irene and smiled weakly.

"Go," she said. "Someone else is coming to help me.

A monstrous ball of flame erupted from the *Hindenburg* as it approached the mooring mast at the Lakehurst airfield.

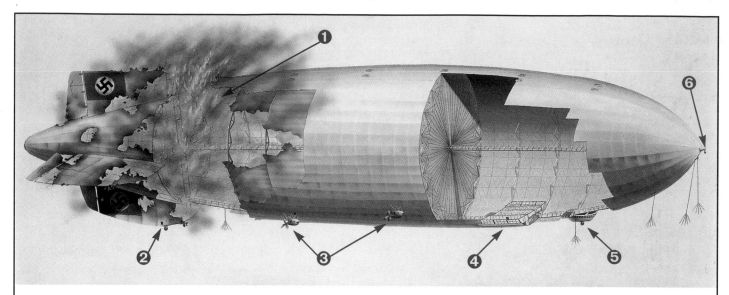

How the Hindenburg burned

The fire started somewhere between gas cells number four and five ❶ and from there spread instantly to the tail of the airship. The zeppelin's tail dropped first and the men in the auxiliary control station were able to run from the ship when the lower fin hit the ground ❷. Many of the mechanics in the engine cars also managed to escape this way ❸. Some of the people in the passenger quarters ❹ and control car ❺ managed to scramble out once the airship was on the ground. Others were trapped inside. The least fortunate aboard were the men in the nose of the ship. As the zeppelin's tail dropped, flames shot through the nose and the airship became a giant torch ❻.

Look, you must go quickly."

With horror, Irene looked up and saw huge flames licking through the back of the room, devouring the carpet, coming straight for her.

"Mother! Father!" she screamed.

"Irene!" Her eyes stinging from the smoke, the girl crawled blindly toward her mother's voice near the windows. She tried to hold her breath, because the room was now filled with smoke and heat. Her hand was especially hot. It was burning up.

Irene opened her eyes and looked at her hand. She was still holding the teddy bear, and the bear was on fire.

The stuffed toy felt as if it were stuck to her, but she finally tore it away. Then she kept moving on her hands and knees in the direction of her mother's voice.

She made it to the window and stood up, clutching her mother's arm. The ground outside seemed unbearably far below them. Bits of the burning ship were peeling off the frame and falling down to the earth like fiery flares.

A man on the ground was shouting at them. He was wearing a white jacket. He looked very small.

"Jump!" he shouted to Irene's mother. "Throw me the kids! I'll catch them! Please hurry!"

Irene looked at her mother, horrified. She couldn't throw the boys out the window. It was too far down. They would break....

"No, Mother, don't — " But her mother had already picked up six-year-old Werner and was holding him out the window. Suddenly Mrs. Doehner squeezed her eyes tightly shut and let go of her son. The man reached out, snatched the boy out of the air and put him on the ground. Then he held up his arms again.

"The other one! Hurry!"

Mrs. Doehner scooped up Walter, but the boy was stiff with fear, and she couldn't lift him.

"Help me, Irene," her mother begged. Together they lifted Walter's legs onto the ledge, and in an instant he was over the side. He landed on top of the man, and the two fell over.

Now the flames were right at Irene's back. She couldn't even look behind her anymore. She climbed over the window ledge and sat on the edge. The ground seemed to be covered with hundreds of bonfires, each one waiting to gobble her up.

She heard a shout beside her. It was Mr. Dolan, the American. He was on the ledge, too.

"It's all right," he shouted. "Look, I'll go first." And he pushed himself off. Irene held her breath, but he landed nimbly on the ground on all fours. It looked easy.

Then, as the man stood up and turned around to wave her down, his arms outstretched, Irene heard a giant cracking sound. As she watched in horror, a flaming metal girder broke away from the ship and collapsed directly on top of him.

Irene turned away, screaming. "I can't do it," she cried to her mother. "I can't jump."

But a second after that she felt a gentle push on her back, and then she was falling.

WERNER FRANZ WAS ALMOST FINISHED PUTTING AWAY the dishes. The rest of the crew had taken their landing positions. He was reaching for another stack of plates when he suddenly lost his footing. It was as if an invisible force had shoved him, hard, against the wall. The dishes rattled briefly and flew out of the cupboard. Cups, saucers, knives and forks rained down on top of him.

The ship trembled and shuddered as Werner leapt for the door to the gangway. What on earth was going on?

"Herr Maier!" he shouted. "Wilhelm!" But there was no answer.

He stumbled out into the hall. It was empty. He seemed to be the only person in this part of the ship. Then

With the flames at her back, Irene prepares to jump from the burning ship.

a hissing roar made him turn around and look down the gangway toward the stern. And what he saw made his throat close up with fear.

A huge flame, bright and terrible, was coming straight for him.

Frantically, Werner started to make his way toward the bow. He managed a few steps, when the ship lurched. The floor slid from beneath him, throwing him onto his stomach. The stern was dropping quickly, and he was sliding backwards, straight into the arms of the blazing fire.

Using all his strength, Werner pulled himself up and crawled along the gangway on his hands and knees. The heat behind him was fierce and close. He could already feel the soles of his shoes burning. Now the fire seemed to be grabbing at his legs ....

A heavy wet blow from above knocked him flat.

Werner didn't know how long he lay there, the breath knocked out of him. Perhaps it was only seconds. But when he next opened his eyes he was lying in a pool of water, his body drenched. One of the water tanks had broken above him.

There was smoke everywhere now. He could barely see. He tried to crawl forward but the slope was too steep. He would never make it to the bow. He was trapped, alone in the ship with the greedy flame still licking at his back.

Then he saw it. The outline of the hatch just beyond reach in front of him. He stretched out his right arm until he thought he would pull it right out of its socket, as his fingers groped for the hatch. The intense heat in the gangway was unbearable. There was only one thing to do.

Without a glance back or another thought, Werner kicked at the hatch with his feet, and jumped.

DEATH OF A GIANT

After the first flames appeared, the fire spread rapidly through the *Hindenburg* (top left) and within half a minute, the great airship was on the ground (bottom left). Many of those on board did not have time to understand what had happened before the fire reached them. But a surprising number of people survived the disaster, like the man above, who was plucked from the white-hot wreckage by the American landing crew. Another fortunate passenger (far right) looks on in horror as the *Hindenburg* burns (right). A rare color photo (top right), shows the Lakehurst landing crew watching helplessly as the giant zeppelin is destroyed by fire.

CHAPTER SIX

The End of a Dream

(Above) Four survivors stumble from the fire. (Left) Captain Pruss was badly burned trying to rescue a fellow officer and had to be taken away by ambulance. After the accident, reporters crowded around (opposite) to learn the names of passengers and crew who had survived. Irene Doehner was listed as alive, but badly burned. She died a few hours later.

WERNER LAY ON THE GROUND WITH his eyes closed and his arms outstretched. For several seconds he wanted to stay there and let the fiery ship wrap around him like a blanket. If he didn't look up, he wouldn't see the flames or see where the screams were coming from. He wouldn't feel the heat and grit from the crumbling zeppelin blowing in his face.

But he knew he had to get up. He pulled himself to his feet. Then he ran out of the fire across the open airfield. At one point he had to skirt around a body lying on the ground. It was so black from burns and smoke that it scarcely looked human. But Werner just kept on running.

He stumbled past a tall figure who pushed past him, going the other way. It was Captain Lehmann. Much of the captain's hair and clothing had been burned off, but still he was heading back into the sea of fire. Werner stopped. It was as if another barrel of water had been thrown in his face.

The passengers. The captain was going back into the ship to try to save more people. To the crew of the *Hindenburg*, the safety of the passengers came first. And Werner was part of that crew.

He turned around and started to run back toward the ship. The giant girders trembled against the brilliant blaze that swallowed up the distant shape of the captain. They seemed to be melting, shrivelling up into nothing. The heat was like a wall, pushing Werner back.

How could anyone survive now? How could he go back into that inferno?

"Hey, kid! Where do you think you're going? Get back here!"

He was grabbed from behind by strong arms. He turned and looked into the stern face of an American naval officer.

"How did you get in here?" the man shouted angrily. "This is no place for a kid!"

Werner didn't understand a word the man was

saying, but he knew from the fierce expression on his face that the officer had no idea who he was. Desperately, the boy searched his brain for the few words of English he knew.

"Cabin boy," he stuttered, pointing to the blazing airship. "Ich bin der Kabinenjunge vom *Hindenburg*. I am the cabin boy of the *Hindenburg*!"

After that, everything became a blur. Werner suddenly felt very cold. His clothes were wet and clinging to his skin, and he was covered in dirt and ash.

The officer led him over to a big low building.

Clustered along the outside wall was a row of news photographers and cameramen. They stood like dolls, their eyes blank. One man pointed his movie camera at the airship and mechanically cranked it by hand. Another shoved slide after slide into his camera, clicking and cocking the shutter in a daze.

Werner turned and looked behind him. The *Hindenburg* was almost unrecognizable. It lay crumpled on the ground, its girders squashed and glowing. It was blazing from end to end, and the silver covering was almost entirely burned off. A giant plume of black smoke billowed from the flames and filled the sky.

The American officer put his own jacket around Werner's shoulders and led him away. As they walked toward the wide hangar doors, one of the photographers lowered his camera from his face. The camera slipped from the man's fingers and fell to the ground with a crack. The photographer didn't even notice. He stood hypnotized by the sight of the airship. His face was as bronze and still as a statue, lit by the reflection of the flames. Then his legs buckled beneath him and he slid to the ground, his back against the wall. He took off his glasses and buried his head in his arms.

Inside the hangar, lights blazed. Sirens sounded in the distance as ambulances began to arrive from the local hospitals. American navy men shouted orders. More and more bodies were carried in and laid on makeshift beds. Some people were whimpering in pain and horror. Others simply stared, their eyes like white moons against their charred faces. Still others, Werner could tell, were dead.

As they walked past a row of bodies, Werner recognized Emmi Imhof, the stewardess. Beside her lay a teenaged girl, her body covered with a blanket.

The girl's eyes were closed, and she was very still.

Sunday, May 9, 1937

WERNER STARED OUT THE CAR WINDOW as Captain Heinen pulled away from his house and headed toward the Lakehurst airfield. Frau Heinen stood on the porch flanked by the family dogs and waved wistfully as Werner waved back. He knew she felt he should stay at home with her instead of spending most of his time at the airfield.

Captain Heinen was a former German airship officer who was stationed in Lakehurst, and he and his family were looking after Werner until he could return to Germany. Frau Heinen spent all day cooking huge German meals and trying hard to make Werner feel at home.

Werner sighed. Frau Heinen reminded him of his mother. He liked her, but she was treating him like a boy,

and he was not a child anymore. That night had changed him. Many of his friends had died, and his ship had been consumed by fire. Yet he had survived, through an amazing stroke of fate. If that water barrel hadn't burst open, drenching him and the flames that were already lapping at his back ....

He knew he would never be the same again. The Heinens were kind, and they wanted to help, but they could never understand what he was feeling. Only someone who had been in that fire, who had survived when others had died, could really understand.

That's why he went back to the airfield every chance he got. He wanted to be with his crewmates — the ones who were left. He needed to be with his airship family.

Most of the men

were staying in quarters at the airfield. Nobody talked much, but Werner didn't care. They needed each other when reports came from the local hospitals on the condition of their crewmates. Captain Pruss had been badly burned, and no one was sure he would live. Willy Speck and Emmi Imhof were dead. Captain Lehmann had died the day after the crash.

Now they were all waiting for the commissions that would investigate the cause of the explosion. Various government and Zeppelin Company officials would be arriving from Germany, including Dr. Hugo Eckener, the president of the Zeppelin Company. Many crew members would have to testify, saying where they had been when the fire started, where they had first seen the flames.

Werner hoped he would not be one of them. He didn't want to relive that night again.

(Top) The day after the disaster, nothing was left of the *Hindenburg* but a smoldering skeleton. This letter, left, sent from Holland, and the burned butter knife, below, were found among the wreckage. Today blackened objects like these are all that remain to remind us of the luxurious life on board the last of the great passenger airships.

"I CAN'T STAND IT IN HERE ANYMORE." WILHELM BALLA swept the chess men off the table in frustration. He and Werner had been staring at the same board for ten minutes.

Werner nodded. Afternoons were always the hardest. By that time they had all played more games of cards and chess and table tennis than they cared to remember.

The Lakehurst staff was friendly and sympathetic, but few of them spoke German. Letters had been written home, and now there was nothing left to do but sit and wait for dinner.

"Come on," Wilhelm said. "Let's go for a walk."

The two wandered outside and without speaking headed toward the twisted metal wreckage in the middle of the airfield. This was all that remained of the *Hindenburg*. Guards had been posted around the ship and nobody was allowed to touch anything. Not that there was much left, anyway. The fire had raged for more than three hours, fed by all the diesel fuel on board. Practically everything had simply burned up. Not even a dish from the officers' mess remained. A few coins and bits of metal lay scattered about, but most things of value were already under lock and key, waiting to be examined by experts.

The sight of the blackened skeleton made Werner choke with sadness and anger.

"What went wrong?" he muttered to Wilhelm. "How could it have happened?"

"Nobody knows," Wilhelm answered in a low voice. He kicked at a reddish stain on the dirt, as one of the guards eyed them suspiciously. "Or if they do, nobody's saying. A lot of the men think there was an electrical charge from the storm, and that it lit some hydrogen that somehow escaped from the back of the ship." He shrugged. "But they're probably just saying that because they don't want to face the real truth."

"What's that?" Werner asked.

Wilhelm looked at him oddly. "You still won't believe it, will you? Zeppelins don't just blow up like that. Somebody caused the explosion. It could have been a bullet shot from the ground. Or maybe it was a time bomb planted by one of the passengers, like that acrobat fellow who was always prowling around the back of the ship, pretending to check on his dog."

"Why would someone on the ship blow it up? It would be just like suicide."

"There are people who are willing to do anything to

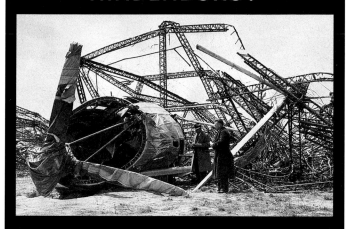

WHAT DESTROYED THE HINDENBURG?

Both the German and American governments inspected the wrecked airship (above) but found no evidence of sabotage. The investigators concluded that the explosion was an accident, caused by hydrogen that escaped from one of the gas cells and was ignited by a spark. The spark might have been caused by one of the metal wires that supported the gas cells snapping as the *Hindenburg* made a sharp turn over the Lakehurst landing field. It is also possible that the spark was the result of static electricity left in the air by the passing storm.

But no fire could have started if the *Hindenburg* had been filled with helium, which does not burn. The disaster of the *Hindenburg* marked the end of the era of ocean crossings by zeppelin. Never again would paying passengers travel aboard a hydrogen-filled airship.

make Hitler look bad," insisted Wilhelm. "Besides, we landed more than twelve hours late. If the *Hindenburg* had been even close to on time, she would have been sitting on the airfield, empty, at the time of the explosion. No one would have been hurt, except Germany. One thing is sure, though, she never would have burned up if the ship had been flying with helium."

The two crewmates stood together and stared at the crumpled pile of metal, all that was left of the great airship. As they turned to go, something solid and brown in the midst of the debris caught Werner's eye.

It was the bust of Paul von Hindenburg that had greeted passengers as they came up the stairs of the ship.

The bust lay on its side, its face half buried in the rubble.

Epilogue

BOTH THE GERMANS AND AMERICANS held inquiries into the causes of the *Hindenburg* disaster. Some people suspected that a crew member or passenger had planted a bomb on the ship. The Zeppelin Company had had bomb scares in the past. The German government had even received a mysterious letter warning that the *Hindenburg* might blow up during a flight to another country.

In the end, though, there was no real evidence to suggest foul play. Most experts believed the fire was a fluke accident, caused by a hydrogen leak that was ignited by a spark from a snapped wire or an electrical charge from the passing storm. All agreed the disaster would not have occurred if the ship had been filled with non-flammable helium instead of hydrogen.

Of the ninety-seven people on board, thirty-five died, including thirteen passengers. But an amazing number of people survived.

Peter Belin smashed a dining-room window with a chair, jumped out and ran to safety. He later became an air pilot.

Joseph Späh, the acrobat, hung from a window sill with one hand, then let go when he was forty feet from the ground. He broke his right ankle in the fall, but was able to crawl away from the ship on his hands and knees. His dog, Ulla, died.

Margaret Mather simply walked out of the ship after it was on the ground, stepping over flickering bits of framework. Her hands were burned and her coat was covered with scorch holes, but she was not permanently injured and she lived to be ninety-eight years old. Throughout the rest of her life, she insisted that she would never hesitate to fly in a zeppelin again.

Mrs. Doehner and her two young sons survived, but Irene Doehner was on fire by the time she jumped. She died in the hospital a few hours later; her father never

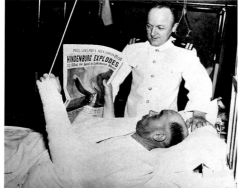

(Opposite) American marines stand at attention in front of the charred frame of the *Hindenburg*. (Above) The American investigation into the explosion found no evidence that foul play was the cause of the disaster.

(Top right) An injured member of the landing crew reads about the end of the *Hindenburg* in his hospital bed. (Above right) The flag-draped coffins of the German victims of the explosion were sent home on a ship from New York.

made it out of the airship. Burt Dolan, whose family did not know he was aboard the *Hindenburg*, was killed by a falling girder. Nelson Morris, who had convinced Dolan to travel on the *Hindenburg*, survived the fire.

There were greater fatalities among the crew. Many crew members who were stationed in the stern were able to jump out of the rear of the ship when the lower tail fin hit the ground. Mechanic Richard Kollmer, who was busy lowering the rear landing wheel when he noticed the fire, was one of the luckiest crew members. As burning cloth fell around him, he jumped from the ship and ran across the airfield. Amazingly, Kollmer was not injured at all.

Crew members at landing positions in the bow were less fortunate. Although the fire started in the stern, flames rushed up through the center of the ship and exploded through the nose, turning the *Hindenburg* into a giant torch. Some men, like Ludwig Knorr, clung to a girder while the stern fell and the bow rose up. When they could hang on no longer, they fell into the blazing inferno. Captain Pruss and Captain Lehmann made it out of the flaming zeppelin,

but both went back into the wreckage several times looking for survivors. Captain Pruss was badly burned trying to rescue Willy Speck, who was trapped in the radio room. In spite of Pruss's bravery, Willy Speck died of his burns. Neither Captain Lehmann nor Emmi Imhof survived.

Werner Franz and Wilhelm Balla were two of the lucky ones. Ten days after the crash, they boarded a steamship and headed back home. Werner arrived in Bremerhaven, Germany, on May 22nd. It was his fifteenth birthday.

Until the crash of the *Hindenburg*, the Zeppelin Company's passenger air service had had a perfect safety record. The company's other big airship, the *Graf Zeppelin*, had been flying across the Atlantic for seven years without a single mishap.

Nevertheless, the *Hindenburg*'s terrible final moments were captured on film by the news people who were on the scene. They had come to cover the fairly routine story of the zeppelin's first 1937 arrival in the United States. They left Lakehurst with photographs and film of the greatest transportation disaster since the sinking of the *Titanic*. A dramatic radio broadcast recorded at the moment of the disaster gave chills to millions of listeners. For the first time in history, photographers were present to record a major tragedy as it happened. By the next day, the horrifying pictures were being shown again and again, in movie theaters and newspapers all over the world. From then on, no one could think of airships without seeing visions of the *Hindenburg* bursting into flames and crashing to the ground.

The Zeppelin Company never recovered from this blow. All future cross-Atlantic flights were canceled. The Americans considered selling Germany helium so airships could fly more safely, but Hitler's moves toward war made them change their minds. Eventually the remaining German zeppelins were dismantled so their metal could be used to make war planes. In 1939, a passenger airplane flew across the Atlantic for the first time, opening up a new era of commercial air travel. Within a few years of the *Hindenburg* disaster, the rigid passenger airship had disappeared from the sky.

In 1937 Richard Kollmer (middle left) was just twenty-two years old and Werner Franz (middle right) only fourteen. But today both Werner (top) and Richard (above) still have vivid memories of the terrifying day nearly sixty years ago when they escaped from the burning *Hindenburg*.

Colorful helium-filled blimps like the Fuji airship (below) have a much smaller control car (right) than the one on the *Hindenburg*. A Goodyear blimp (above and opposite) was flown over Florida to flash messages to people left without electricity after a hurricane.

Today we only see smaller helium-filled blimps — like the airship Jim Hain and his team use — nonrigid gas bags that are used most often as flying billboards to advertise a company name during sports events. But people are beginning to realize that airships have other uses, too. Capable of hovering like helicopters, they are cheaper to fly and maintain, make less noise, don't create a downdraft, and can stay in the air for longer periods of time.

A blimp inflated with hot air was recently used to carry a light rubber raft over an African rainforest and gently place it on the highest branches. This raft, filled with research equipment, allowed scientists to live in the treetops and gather new information about the rainforest.

New ways to take advantage of the airship's unique capabilities are being devised all the time. When Hurricane Andrew left parts of southern Florida without telephones or electricity in September 1992, a blimp flew overhead flashing vital messages to people who had no other means of receiving news from the rest of the world.

Airships equipped with sophisticated cameras and scanning devices have been used by police forces to keep an eye on crowds and traffic over entire cities. They can

patrol border crossings to prevent smuggling, watch over crowded shipping lanes (where accidents happen daily) and track oil spills from above.

A modern zeppelin could be even better than the *Hindenburg*. By using space-age electrical and computer equipment, it would be possible to save manpower and weight. High-tech radar could detect changes in the weather early enough to help the airship avoid storms. Space-age fabrics and metal alloys are lighter and stronger than the materials used in the *Hindenburg*, while modern engines and propellers could provide improved handling and maneuvering capabilities.

One day we may see giant airships soaring above the clouds, where they can take advantage of the two greatest sources of cheap, pollution-free energy — the sun and the wind. An airship's huge reflective surface could be covered with solar panels.

Building a space-age airship is risky and expensive; but so is any brave new invention. Like Count von Zeppelin, today's airship engineers face setbacks and skepticism while they work toward their goal. With enough enthusiasm and support, though, they may well prove that the great airship adventure has not come to an end, but is only beginning.

GLOSSARY

ballast: The water stored in tanks inside a zeppelin which could be dropped to make the ship lighter. Dropping ballast would cause the ship to rise higher.

blimp: A non-rigid airship, inflated with helium, which gets its shape from the pressure of the gas that fills it. Because it has no internal frame, if it is not inflated a blimp will collapse like a balloon.

Buster Brown: A velvet suit with short pants.

DC-3: A type of plane flown in the 1930s.

dirigible: Any airship that is driven by an engine and can be steered through the sky. Zeppelins and blimps are both dirigibles. But hot-air balloons, since they are driven by the wind, are not dirigibles.

elevator man: The member of a zeppelin's crew who was responsible for keeping the nose of the ship level as it flew. The elevator man's job was one of the most difficult and important on the ship.

Frau: The German word for "Mrs."

Fräulein: The German word for "Miss."

gangway: A name for the halls or passages on a zeppelin.

gondola: The car that is attached to the outside of a blimp or zeppelin.

hangar: The enormous building where a zeppelin was constructed and housed between flights.

helium: The second lightest gas known. Colorless, non-flammable helium is used to inflate modern blimps.

Herr: The German word for "Mr."

Hitler, Adolf: The leader of the Nazi party and dictator of Germany from 1933 to 1945. His racist beliefs and military aggression brought suffering and death to millions.

hydrogen: The lightest gas known. Hydrogen is colorless, odorless and extremely flammable.

Jawohl: German for "yes."

John Keats: An English poet who lived from 1795 to 1821. He lived in Rome for the last four months of his short life.

landing lines: The 400-foot-long ropes dropped from a zeppelin's nose when it reached a landing field. Men on the ground could haul the zeppelin to earth by pulling on the ropes.

Luftwaffe: The German air force.

mess: The room where the zeppelin's crew ate their meals.

mooring mast: The steel tower to which the nose of a zeppelin was attached after it landed.

Nazi: A member of the political party that controlled Germany from 1933 to 1945. The Nazi party was led during those years by Adolf Hitler.

payload: A name for the paying cargo carried on a zeppelin. This did not include the passengers' luggage.

Reich: The German empire. The Nazi era (1933 to 1945) is often referred to as the Third Reich.

Reichsmark: The money used in Germany from 1925 to 1948.

rigger: One of the members of a zeppelin's crew responsible for checking the ship's outer covering for holes or tears and watching for leaks in the gas cells.

Sorbonne: A part of the University of Paris.

steerage: In passenger ships the poorest people were housed on the lower decks near the rudder in an area known as "the steerage."

steward: One of the members of a zeppelin's crew responsible for serving food and looking after the passengers.

swastika: A symbol used by the Nazis shaped like a cross with four arms of equal length bending at right angles in a clockwise direction.

zeppelin: A rigid airship made of an aluminum frame containing gas cells inflated with a lighter-than-air gas. A zeppelin gets its shape from its internal frame and will keep this shape whether its gas cells are inflated or not.

TWO HUNDRED YEARS OF LIGHTER-THAN-AIR FLIGHT

1783 At the palace of the king and queen of France, Joseph and Etienne Montgolfier demonstrate their new invention, a huge cloth balloon filled with hot air. The balloon, carrying a rooster, a sheep and a duck in its basket, rises into the air and flies for eight minutes.

1898 Alberto Santos-Dumont equips his balloon with a modified motorcycle engine and a rudder and can then direct its flight in any direction he chooses. But the tiny ship can carry only one person at a time and Santos-Dumont uses it to tour Paris and explore the French countryside.

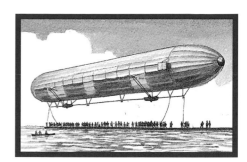

1900 Germany's Count Ferdinand von Zeppelin places bags of hydrogen gas inside an enormous cloth-covered metal frame and creates an airship that can be steered through the skies. Zeppelins, as the huge airships are named, will carry passengers on sightseeing trips across Germany.

1914-18 During the First World War, German zeppelins are used to bomb London from the air. Though their bombs damage English cities, the zeppelins often fly off course, miss their targets or are shot down by British planes. By the end of the war, so many German zeppelins have been lost that the airships are declared useless as war machines.

1926 Roald Amundsen, the first man to reach the South Pole, buys an airship from the Italians and puts Umberto Nobile, the airship's designer, in command. These two men and their crew are the first people ever to fly over the North Pole. They travel from Spitsbergen, Norway, to Teller, Alaska, covering a distance of 3,180 miles in 70 hours, 40 minutes.

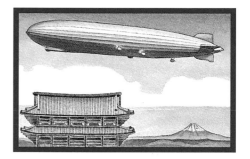

1929 The German airship *Graf Zeppelin* carries 20 passengers on the first non-stop flight around the world. The *Graf* passes over uncharted parts of eastern Siberia and stops briefly in Japan before flying on to Los Angeles. It then crosses America and returns to Germany in triumph. The age of international passenger travel by zeppelin has begun.

1937 On May 6, the *Hindenburg*, the largest and most luxurious zeppelin ever to fly, explodes and crashes to the ground at Lakehurst, New Jersey, killing 35 of the 97 people aboard. News of the disaster horrifies the world and hydrogen-filled airships are never again used to transport paying passengers.

1939-45 The United States Navy uses non-flammable helium to inflate its observation blimps. These blimps fly above the navy's ships during the Second World War and watch for enemy submarines. Not a single ship under the protection of the navy blimps is ever sunk by an enemy submarine.

1993 Blimps' slow speed and their ability to hover quietly for long periods make them the ideal platform for marine biologist Jim Hain to observe whales. His research will help us to learn more about the whales' migration routes and their feeding, swimming and diving behavior.

RECOMMENDED FURTHER READING

Blimps

by Roxie Munro — 1989 (E.P. Dutton, U.S.)
This book by *New Yorker* artist Roxie Munro takes readers for a ride in a modern blimp and explains how today's airships are made, manned, maneuvered and moored.

Lighter Than Air: An Illustrated History of the Airship

by Lee Payne — 1991 (Orion, U.S.)
Payne traces the development of lighter-than-air flight from the first experiments of the Montgolfier brothers to the great rigid airships, the U.S. Navy blimps, and the present-day uses of lighter-than-air craft.

The Giant Airships

by Douglas Botting and the editors of Time-Life Books — 1981 (Time-Life Books, U.S.)
Follows the careers of the best-known rigid airships and the men who designed and flew them.

The Golden Age of the Great Passenger Airships: Graf Zeppelin and Hindenburg

by Harold G. Dick with Douglas H. Robinson — *1985* (Smithsonian Institution Press, U.S., U.K.)
Leading airship historians Dick and Robinson present a thorough technical examination of Germany's best-known passenger zeppelins.

NEW-YORK

RIO DE JANEIRO